CHRISTOPHER COLUMBUS
Great Explorer

CHRISTOPHER COLUMBUS

Great Explorer

A FIRST BIOGRAPHY

by DAVID A. ADLER

illustrated by Lyle Miller

Holiday House/New York

IMPORTANT DATES

1451	Born in Genoa, Italy.
1476	The *Bechalla* sank. Columbus swam ashore in Lagos, Portugal.
1479	Married Dona Felipa Perestrello e Moniz.
1480	Birth of first son, Diego.
1484–1492	Tried to find a royal sponsor for his journey west to the Indies.
1485	Left Portugal to live in Spain after the death of Dona Felipa.
1488	Birth of second son, Ferdinand, to Columbus and Beatrice Enríquez de Harana.
1492	Left Palos, Spain, on August 3 for first voyage across Atlantic Ocean.
1492	Landed in America on October 12.
1492	After *Santa María* shipwrecked on December 25, colony of Hispaniola founded.
1493	Returned to Palos, Spain.
1493–1496	Second voyage west across the Atlantic.
1498–1500	Third voyage, after which Columbus returned to Portugal in chains.
1502–1504	Fourth voyage.
1506	Died at Valladolid, Spain, on May 20.

CONTENTS

1. A Boy with Dreams

CHRISTOPHER COLUMBUS was born in Genoa in the fall of 1451. To people in Genoa and elsewhere in Europe, the world seemed smaller then. They thought there was one huge body of land— Europe, Africa, and Asia—broken by various seas and surrounded by one great body of water, the Ocean Sea.

The Atlantic Ocean, the large body of water to the west of Portugal, was called the Sea of Darkness. The legends surrounding it were frightening. Sailors told tales of bubbling, boiling water and of giant sea monsters. People in Europe didn't know of the land and people living on the other side of the Atlantic.

Genoa was a great port city at the shore of the Ligurian Sea, part of the Mediterranean Sea. It was an independent city-state in the northwest of what would one day be Italy. But Italy had not been founded yet. Sailing west from Genoa harbor would lead through the Strait of Gibraltar to the Atlantic Ocean. Young Christopher often sat at the harbor in Genoa. He listened to sailors tell of their experiences at sea. He stared at the tall masts and sails of the many boats tied up there, breathed in the warm, salty air, and dreamed of sailing on the open water.

In Genoa, narrow cobblestone alleyways led up from the water. The city was surrounded by walls built to protect the city from enemies. For a few years, Christopher's father, Domenico, was a keeper of one of the gates in the wall.

Domenico and his wife Susanna were married in 1445, six years before Christopher was born. It's possible they had other children before Christopher, but if they did, the children did not survive. Medicine was primitive in the fifteenth century, and it was common for infants to die soon after they were born.

The exact date of Christopher's birth is not known. Perhaps even Christopher did not know the date and never celebrated his own birthday. Instead it's likely he celebrated the feast day of his patron saint, Saint Christopher.

Christopher had three brothers and a sister. One of the boys died young. His other brothers were Bartholomew, who was close in age to Christopher, and Diego, who was seventeen years younger. Their sister's name was Bianchetta.

Domenico and his wife, Susanna, were the children of wool weavers. Domenico was a wool weaver, too, and he expected that his eldest child, Christopher, would also become one.

Christopher and Bartholomew helped their father. They combed raw wool to clean it and untangle the fibers. Their mother spun the wool into yarn. Domenico worked the loom and wove the yarn into cloth. They worked as long as there was daylight. At night they slept on cloth bags filled with straw. They lived in a simple stone house with wooden shutters on the windows to keep out the cold. They had a table, benches, and a chest or two.

Christopher was a tall boy with a long face, red hair, and freckles. He hated the life of a wool weaver. Whenever he could, he boarded a boat. Sometimes his father sent him across the sea to buy raw wool, wine, and cheese, and to sell the finished cloth from his loom. Christopher also took short fishing trips, but he rarely went so far from shore that he lost sight of land.

Christopher dreamed of sailing in the open, unknown water beyond the Strait of Gibraltar. He dreamed not only of the adventure of the voyage, but of the riches it would bring him.

Explorers along the African coast became wealthy from trading beads, bells, cloth, and horses for pepper, ivory, gold, and slaves. But the best place for trade was in faraway lands to the east.

Christopher read of Marco Polo who traveled across Asia to China from 1271–1274. He returned to Italy twenty-four years later with a fortune in jewels, silk, and ivory. People still spoke of the riches in the East, but in 1453, when Christopher was two years old, Muslim Turks conquered Constantinople. The land route to China and the Indies was dangerous for Christians. Perhaps somewhere, across the ocean, was another route to the riches of the East.

2. The Spirit of Adventure

IN MAY 1476, when Christopher Columbus was twenty-four, he had his first great adventure at sea. He boarded the *Bechalla*, one of five trading ships carrying cargo bound for Portugal, England, and Flanders. The ships sailed together, armed to protect themselves from enemies and pirates. After they passed the Strait of Gibraltar, they were suddenly attacked. A much larger fleet of ships led by Guillaume de Casenove, a famous French pirate, surrounded them.

The Italian merchant sailors and the pirates fought all day with cannon and fire. Seven ships sank, including four pirate ships and the *Bechalla*. Hundreds of men died in the battle. Many died in the fires or by drowning when they jumped overboard. Columbus was injured, and as his ship was going down, he dove into the water. He grabbed onto a long oar which had floated free from the wreckage and swam six miles to shore in Lagos, Portugal.

It was either great luck or fate that brought Columbus ashore in Portugal. It was the center in Europe for brave seamen intent on exploration. And Lagos, where Columbus rested and recovered from his injuries, was only a few miles from Sagres, the home of Prince Henry the Navigator.

Prince Henry was the son of the king and queen of Portugal. He had gathered mathematicians, geographers, mapmakers, and astronomers in Sagres, where he had set up an observatory. He financed the development of better instruments for sailing and sent out more than fifty voyages of exploration along the western coast of Africa. He died sixteen years before Columbus dove off the *Bechalla* and swam ashore, but the spirit of adventure remained strong in Portugal.

As soon as Columbus was able to travel, he went north to Lisbon, the capital city of Portugal. He lived there off and on for eight years. The time he spent in Lisbon changed him from a poor, ignorant sailor to a man with great ideas and a knowledge of the world. It was there that Columbus decided to sail west to reach the rich lands of the East.

He went to Ireland, Iceland, and the Azores on a merchant ship. A few years later he joined a sailing crew sent by the king of Portugal on a long voyage along the coast of Africa. He sailed with experienced seamen and learned from them what to take along for a long voyage, how to sail in all kinds of weather, and to depend on the ship and God to get him through the fiercest storm.

When Columbus was not off sailing somewhere, he explored Lisbon. It was a busy, exciting city with brightly painted houses, narrow streets, and small shops. One of the shops, where books and maps were sold, belonged to Christopher's brother, Bartholomew. There, Bartholomew and Christopher made maps for sailors.

In 1479, while attending church in Lisbon, Christopher met Dona Felipa Perestrello e Moniz, a young woman from a prominent family. Her father was one of the explorers who discovered the Madeira Islands in the Atlantic six hundred miles west of Lisbon. He had studied navigation with Prince Henry. Christopher and Dona Felipa were married and in 1480 had a son, Diego.

3.   Finally, a Sponsor

In 1484, Christopher Columbus made his first attempt to interest a king in providing him with the ships, crew, and provisions he would need for making a voyage west across the Atlantic. He presented his plan to King John II of Portugal, the grandnephew of Prince Henry the Navigator. Traveling west to reach the East wasn't Columbus's idea alone, nor was he the first to present it to the king, but he was the first to petition to lead the voyage.

Columbus did not have to convince King John that the East Indies could be reached by sailing west. It was well-known that the earth was a sphere. But how long a journey would it be? Could enough food and water be taken aboard to sustain the seamen? Columbus thought he would have to sail 2,400 miles west from the Azores to reach Japan. Actually, the distance to Japan is more than four times as long.

Columbus spoke with great confidence. He was a tall and handsome man. The king's advisers listened, but they thought his numbers were wrong, that Japan was much farther away. They refused to sponsor him.

In 1485, the same year that King John turned him down, Columbus's wife, Dona Felipa, died. Soon after her death, Columbus and his five-year-old son Diego left Portugal for Spain. Diego stayed at a monastery in Palos, Spain, while Columbus looked for someone to provide him with the ships and men he would need for his voyage west. While he was in Spain, Columbus lived with a young peasant woman, Beatriz Enríquez de Harana. Their son, Ferdinand, was born in 1488.

In 1486, Columbus met with the king and queen of Spain, Ferdinand and Isabella. He asked for the ships and seamen that he needed and to be rewarded if he found a sea route to the East. He wanted to be named Admiral of the Ocean Sea, made governor of all the lands he found, and given a share of the riches he brought back. Queen Isabella did not give Columbus a definite answer. She appointed a commission to consider the matter.

Christopher Columbus spent the next six years trying to find someone to sponsor the voyage. He traveled back to Portugal to ask King John again, and Christopher's brother Bartholomew petitioned Prince Henry VII of England and King Charles VIII of France. All three kings refused to provide the ships and men. Then, in January 1492, after long consideration, King Ferdinand and Queen Isabella of Spain gave Columbus a definite answer: No.

Columbus left the Spanish royal court. He was on his way to petition King Charles of France again. But after he left, the discussion at court continued. An adviser to Ferdinand and Isabella pointed out that the cost of the voyage was relatively small. The king and queen often spent more for one week's entertainment. And the rewards of such a trip could be huge. If Columbus succeeded, he could set up a Spanish trading post in the East and bring back lots of gold, silks, and spices. Queen Isabella agreed and even offered to sell her crown jewels to help pay for the voyage. She quickly sent a messenger to bring Columbus back. He finally had a sponsor and could prepare for his great adventure.

4. The *Niña, Pinta,* and *Santa María*

CHRISTOPHER COLUMBUS went to Palos, Spain, to find the ships and recruit the men for the voyage. The ships he chose were the *Niña,* the *Pinta,* and the *Santa María.* In Palos he also found the ninety men he needed to sail with him.

Each boat had a captain on board, a pilot, a doctor, a boatswain who checked the ropes and sails, a steward who had charge of the food, and a caulker who kept the boat from leaking. A secretary went along to keep a record of the voyage and an accountant to make sure the king and queen would receive their share of the gold and other riches Columbus might find. He also had a silversmith who knew the value of rare metals and minerals, and an interpreter who spoke Hebrew and Arabic.

The men generally wore parkas with a hood, red woolen stocking caps, and no shoes. On board they hardly washed their clothes or bathed, and they didn't shave. They ate dry biscuits, cheese, dried beans, chick-peas, lentils, rice, salted fish, and meat. They drank water and plenty of wine. At night they slept on deck if the weather was good, and belowdecks if it was not. But they weren't alone down there. With them in the dampness were cockroaches, worms, and rats.

The three ships left the harbor on August 3, 1492. The day before, August second, was the deadline for another group of voyagers. Ferdinand and Isabella had set that date for all Jews who refused to be baptized as Christians to leave Spain or be executed. Tens of thousands of Jews whose families had lived in Spain for hundreds of years crowded Spanish harbors and boarded ships for Portugal, North Africa, Italy, and Turkey. Columbus may have waited until August third to avoid sailing off among the shiploads of banished Jews.

The *Niña*, *Pinta*, and the *Santa María* sailed south to the
Canary Islands and reached them in nine days. There the crew
took aboard more meat, cheese, and fresh water. The *Pinta* had
its rudder repaired and on September 6, 1492, the ships sailed
west into unknown waters.

Christopher Columbus prayed regularly and often observed
religious fasts. He wouldn't curse other than to say, on occa-
sion, ''By San Fernando,'' and ''May God take you.'' He was
sure of himself and certain that on this voyage he would reach
the East. But Columbus knew that his men were not so confi-
dent. He knew that after a while, they might become impatient
to find land, so he kept two records of the distance traveled. He
kept a true record for himself and another one that showed they
were not nearly so far from home. He let the men see the second
record so that they wouldn't become too discouraged.

They had a steady wind for ten days and then it rained and the waves became rough. About three weeks into the voyage, the men began to complain. They were bored, tired, and probably frightened. During the past few weeks they had seen nothing but water, sky, and each other. They wanted to turn back. Columbus refused. For years he had dreamed of this journey and little else. He had planned for it, and petitioned kings to send him. He wouldn't turn back now.

By October 6, they had sailed more than 2,400 miles. According to Columbus's original reckoning they should have already reached Japan. On October 7, they saw a large flock of birds fly overhead. Columbus changed his course and followed the birds. By October 11, they saw leaves and branches floating in the water, a sure sign that land was nearby.

Then, at two hours past midnight on Friday, October 12, Rodrigo de Triana, a seaman on the *Pinta,* saw something in the moonlight. *"Tierra! Tierra!"* he called out. "Land! Land!"

A cannon was fired to alert the other ships. Men ran onto the deck to look. They saw a small island, one of the Bahamas, six miles ahead. The men shouted and sang. They prayed and cried for joy.

By morning, the boats had reached the island. Christopher Columbus and some men went ashore. Columbus claimed the island for the king and queen of Spain. He named it San Salvador.

The natives watched Columbus and his men. To them the men looked pale. The natives were surprised at the clothing Columbus and the others wore and the strange words they spoke.

Columbus looked at the natives and saw a quiet, gentle, and seemingly peaceful people. He saw mostly tall, strong-looking young men who were naked. Some had faces that were painted red, black, and white, and others were completely covered with paint. They didn't carry knives or spears or weapons of any kind. When they saw the swords Columbus and his men held, they reached out to hold them. But they didn't know how to handle a sword. They grabbed onto the blades and cut themselves. Columbus was sure he had reached the Indies, so he called the people he met there Indians.

Columbus described the Indians in a letter as a generous people, willing to share with him anything they had. They appreciated the glass beads and tiny bells he gave them, as if they were some great treasure. Columbus decided that the Indians could be easily converted to Christianity and just as easily made into obedient servants.

The arrival of Columbus was a tragic happening for the Indians. Europeans brought unknown diseases with them. Indians were captured by the thousands and forced into slavery. Many of them committed suicide rather than be taken to Europe. In the years ahead, millions of Indians would be brutally killed by the conquering people from across the ocean.

Columbus stayed on San Salvador for two days and explored the island. Then, on October 14, he took six natives with him to be his guides and interpreters and sailed farther west. He went from island to island, hoping to find the mainland of China or Japan or, at the very least, some gold.

On December 25, the *Santa María* was caught on a reef off the coast of an island and wrecked. Columbus decided that this was an omen. God meant him to found a settlement there—and he did. He called the island Hispaniola.

Indians helped Columbus unload the ship. With the wood they saved from the sinking *Santa María,* the crew built a fort. Forty men stayed to search for gold. On January 16, 1493, Columbus and some fifty men set sail on the *Niña* and the *Pinta* for home.

There was rough sailing on the return voyage. During the second week in February, the men encountered strong winds, rain, and lightning. The boats were thrown around in the water. Great waves broke across the decks. Columbus was afraid that the ships and all the men aboard would be lost. Then there would be no record of his voyage. In the midst of the storm, he wrote some notes on parchment. He sealed them in a barrel and threw it overboard. He hoped that if he and everything else were lost, at least these notes would prove that he had reached the Indies.

On February 14 the sky cleared and the sea became calm. A month later the *Niña* and the *Pinta* arrived safely in Palos, Spain. But the barrel with Columbus's notes on the voyage was never found.

Columbus sent word to King Ferdinand and Queen Isabella in Barcelona that he had reached the Indies and returned safely. Then he traveled to Barcelona with some of his men. He also took along parrots in cages and six Indians. When Columbus arrived at the royal court, the king and queen rose from their thrones to greet him, a great honor. They even asked Columbus to sit with them. He did, and he told them about the voyage.

Christopher Columbus was a hero. People crowded the roads to see this great explorer and the strange people, the Indians, he brought from the East. King Ferdinand and Queen Isabella named Columbus *Admiral of the Ocean Sea* and *Viceroy of the Indies*. He stayed in Barcelona, talked about his great journey, and planned a second voyage to the New World.

5. Trouble in Hispaniola

ON SEPTEMBER 25, 1493, Christopher Columbus set sail again. His brother Diego went along this time. They sailed west with what Columbus called a "handsome fleet" of seventeen ships and about twelve hundred men.

The object of this voyage was to settle Hispaniola. Farmers went on the voyage with seeds to plant in the New World. There were cows on the ships and sheep and horses, too. Six priests planned to convert the Indians.

The ships docked briefly in the Canary Islands, took on more food and fresh water, and then sailed west. By November 3, they reached islands in the Caribbean Sea. They tasted pineapple for the first time and found evidence of a tribe of Indians who ate human flesh.

On November 27, Columbus came to Hispaniola. A cannon was fired to announce to the forty men who had settled there ten months before that Columbus had returned. There was no answer to the cannon fire because all forty men were dead. They had been cruel to the Indians, and the Indians had killed them. The fort had been burned.

Columbus sailed to the northern coast of Hispaniola and founded a new colony there. He named it Isabela after the queen. It was a poor place for a settlement. There was no fresh water nearby, and it was swarming with mosquitoes. Hundreds of men became sick, and there was not nearly enough medicine for them all. There was not enough food, either, and the men wouldn't eat the squash and corn that the Indians ate.

Columbus sent twelve ships to Spain loaded with parrots, wood, a little gold, and many Indian slaves. He wanted the ships sent back with food and medicine. The slaves on board did not fare well. Many died during the voyage. Others arrived ashore too sick to work.

Columbus explored Cuba and Jamaica. When he returned to Isabela, he found chaos. His men were fighting among themselves and with the Indians. Unhappy sailors had taken three ships and sailed home.

Some relief ships from Spain had arrived in Isabela with supplies and with Christopher's brother Bartholomew. He told Christopher that the men who had gone back to Spain were speaking badly of him, complaining about how he was ruling the island and that there was no gold.

Columbus returned to Spain on June 11, 1496. He went to see the king and queen and brought along some Indian slaves wearing fancy feather headdresses and gold jewelry. He gave Ferdinand and Isabella some gold nuggets. He told them about his new discoveries and asked them to please send him back. They did, and on May 30, 1498, Columbus began his third voyage to the New World.

He took six ships with him from Spain. Three left the Canary Islands directly for the settlement in Hispaniola. Columbus sailed with the other three farther south and then west. It was a difficult journey. For more than a week there was no wind to push the sails. The heat was so great that Columbus described it as a fire. Food spoiled. Barrels of water and wine burst apart. Finally, the ships reached an island with three mountains off the coast of South America. Columbus named it Trinidad. A few days later they sailed along the eastern coast of South America. The natives were friendly there. They wore large pieces of jewelry made with gold and huge pearl necklaces. Columbus traded for some pearls and planned to return for more. He never did.

Columbus sailed north for Hispaniola and arrived there on August 31, 1498. His brother Bartholomew told him of all the troubles in the settlement. Many of the settlers were sick. There had been fights with the Indians. Spanish settlers rebelled and joined the Indians in the battles against the rule of the Columbus brothers.

Columbus tried to calm the rebellion. He allowed settlers to return to Spain. Those who remained in the New World were given land.

There was trouble for Columbus in Spain, too. Settlers who had returned continued to complain about conditions in the New World. They demanded that the king pay them for all the time they had spent there. In Spain, Columbus was known as the ''Admiral of the Mosquitoes.''

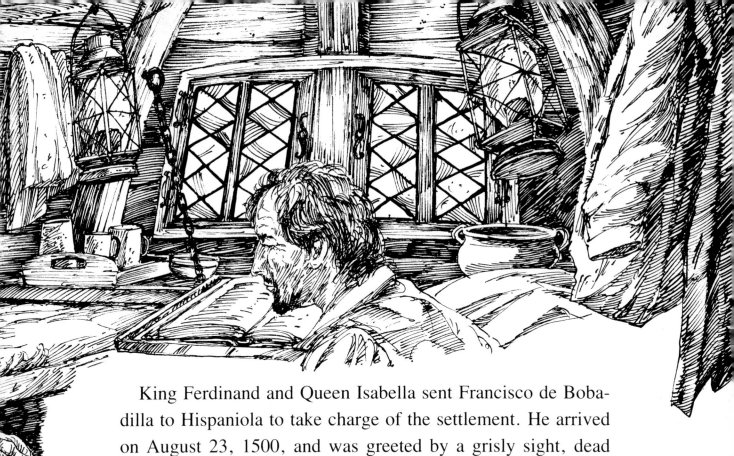

King Ferdinand and Queen Isabella sent Francisco de Bobadilla to Hispaniola to take charge of the settlement. He arrived on August 23, 1500, and was greeted by a grisly sight, dead Spanish settlers hanging from a gallows. Bobadilla was shocked. He put the Columbus brothers, Christopher, Bartholomew, and Diego, in chains and sent them back to Spain.

While crossing the Atlantic, the captain offered to release Christopher. Columbus refused. The king and queen ordered the chains to be removed, but Christopher wouldn't give them up. He kept them to remind him of his disgrace and even asked that when he died, the chains be buried with him.

Gold and pearls were coming back from the New World. King Ferdinand and Queen Isabella realized the great value of Christopher Columbus's discoveries and allowed him to sail again, his fourth and final voyage to the New World, but they warned him not to stop at Hispaniola until he was on his way home.

6.   A Great Seaman

CHRISTOPHER COLUMBUS sailed on May 9, 1502, with a crew of mostly inexperienced sailors in four old ships. His brother Bartholomew and his son Ferdinand sailed with him. Columbus would search for a water passageway into the Indian Ocean.

Columbus stopped off at Martinique and then sailed toward Hispaniola. He was sure a hurricane was coming. He sent someone ashore to warn the new governor of Hispaniola about the storm. He asked permission to tie his boats up and go ashore with his men until the bad weather passed. The governor refused to allow Columbus to dock on the island, and he laughed at his warning. What did Columbus know about storms? The governor had planned to send a large fleet of ships to Spain the very next day, and he did.

Since Columbus was no longer welcome in Hispaniola, the governor was sending Columbus's belongings back to Spain. Francisco de Bobadilla, who had put Christopher in chains just two years earlier, was on one of the ships. The rest of the ships carried gold and other cargo. Soon after the fleet left the harbor, the storm hit. More than twenty ships were lost or sank. More than five hundred men were drowned, including Bobadilla. Four ships came back to the harbor too damaged to go on. Only one ship, the *Aguja,* survived the storm and made it to Spain. This was the ship carrying the belongings of Christopher Columbus.

Columbus was prepared for the storm. All four of his ships survived it. None of his men were lost.

For the next year, Columbus sailed in the Caribbean along the coast of Central America. After a year of sailing, the bottoms of the old boats were being eaten by worms. Weevils were eating the provisions. Sometimes the hungry men ate only in the dark so they wouldn't see the tiny animals crawling on their food. Columbus reached Jamaica in June 1503, but the old boats could sail no farther. He sent a few men to the governor of Hispaniola and asked for help.

Eight months later Columbus and his men were still waiting in Jamaica. Their food had run out and the Indians were tired of feeding Columbus and his always-hungry men. According to his son Ferdinand, who had gone along, each Spanish sailor could eat as much food as twenty Indians.

Columbus knew an eclipse of the moon was coming on the night of February 29. That afternoon he told the Indians that God was angry with them for not providing his men with enough to eat. At night, when the moon seemed to disappear in the sky, the Indians were frightened. Columbus told them this was a warning from God. They should take better care of the Spanish sailors. After that, the Indians gave the men plenty of food. Four months later, a small ship was finally sent from Hispaniola, and Columbus and his men sailed for home.

Columbus returned to Spain on November 7, 1504. He was fifty-three years old. He had been at sea for most of the past twelve years. He was tired and sick. He had arthritis and it was hard for him to move around. About three weeks after his return to Spain, on November 26, 1504, Queen Isabella, his champion in the royal court, died.

Columbus felt he wasn't getting his share of the gold and trade coming from the New World. He complained to King Ferdinand. Columbus was given an income, but it was not as much as he felt he deserved. Still, it was enough to make him a rich man.

Christopher Columbus became quite ill and stayed mostly in his bed in a small house in Valladolid, Spain. His sons Diego and Ferdinand, his brother Diego, and a few friends were with him on Wednesday, May 20, 1506, when he died. He was fifty-four years old.

Christopher Columbus was a strong-willed, determined man and a great seaman. He died still believing he had reached the East. He hadn't, but the voyages he made had changed the world. He linked Europe and America. He began a great era of exploration. His bravery at sea and his discoveries encouraged others to sail to unknown lands.

INDEX

To Sheila Miller, a dynamic school librarian

Text copyright © 1991 by David A. Adler

Illustrations copyright © 1991 by Lyle Miller

Printed in the United States of America

First Edition

Library of Congress Cataloging-in-Publication Data
Adler, David A.
Christopher Columbus : great explorer / David A. Adler :
illustrations by Lyle Miller.
p. cm.
Summary: Chronicles the life, voyages, and discoveries of the
intrepid explorer.
ISBN 0-8234-0895-7
1. Columbus, Christopher—Juvenile literature.
2. America—Discovery and exploration—Spanish—Juvenile
literature. 3. Explorers—Spain—Biography—
Juvenile literature. 4. Explorers—America—Biography—
Juvenile literature. [1. Columbus, Christopher. 2. Explorers.
3. America—Discovery and exploration—
Spanish.] I. Miller, Lyle, 1950–   ill. II. Title.
E111.A26 1991
970.01'5'092—dc20   90-28668   CIP   AC
[B]
[92]